SEQUENCE AND SERIES

NCEA Level 2 Internal

Charlotte Walker and Victoria Walker

Walker Maths 2.3 Sequence and Series
1st Edition
Charlotte Walker
Victoria Walker

Editor: Eva Chan
Cover and text design: Cheryl Smith, Macarn Design
Production controller: Siew Han Ong
Reprint: Jess Lovell

Acknowledgements
Cover photo courtesy of Shutterstock.

For product information and technology assistance,
in Australia call **1300 790 853**;
in New Zealand call **0800 449 725**

For permission to use material from this text or product, please email
aust.permissions@cengage.com

National Library of New Zealand Cataloguing-in-Publication Data
A catalogue record for this book is available from the National Library of New Zealand.

ISBN 978 017 0 354202

Cengage Learning Australia
Level 7, 80 Dorcas Street
South Melbourne, Victoria Australia 3205

For learning solutions, visit **cengage.co.nz**

Printed in China by 1010 Printing International Ltd
17 25

CONTENTS

ISBN: 9780170354202

Formulae

These are the formulae for this achievement standard. Remember to check with your teacher to see which ones you will be provided with in your assessment.

Arithmetic general term	$t_n = a + (n-1)d$
Sum of arithmetic sequences	$S_n = \frac{n}{2}[2a + (n-1)d]$ $= \frac{n[2a + (n-1)d]}{2}$
Geometric general term	$t_n = a \times r^{n-1}$
Sum of geometric sequences	$S_n = \frac{a(1-r^n)}{(1-r)}$
Sum to infinity	$S_\infty = \frac{a}{(1-r)}$

ISBN: 9780170354202

Glossary

Make your own glossary of key terms:

Term	Definition	Picture/Example
Sequence		
Series		
First term (a)		
Common difference (d)		
Term number (n)		
Common ratio (r)		
Arithmetic		
Geometric		
Infinity		
Sum		
Consecutive		
Depreciate		

ISBN: 9780170354202

Arithmetic sequences

An arithmetic sequence is one in which each term is calculated by adding or subtracting the same number each time. There is a common difference, *d*, between consecutive terms.

Example:

+4 +4 +4 +4

2, 6, 10, 14, 18, …

The common difference, *d*, for this sequence is 4, because 4 is added each time. The next three terms in the sequence would be:

+4 +4 +4

2, 6, 10, 14, 18, **22, 26, 30**

Find the next three terms in these sequences.

1 1, 6, 11, 16, 21, …

2 23, 18, 13, 8, …

3 3, 6, 9, 12, 15, …

4 7, 11, 15, 19, 23, …

5 120, 110, 100, 90, …

6 11, 4, -3, -10, …

7 0.5, 1.0, 1.5, 2.0, 2.5, …

8 18, 27, 36, 45, 54, …

9 5, 3, 1, -1, -3, …

10 ½, ¾, 1, 1¼, …

11 5, 5.5, 6, 6.5, 7, …

12 0.3, 0.2, 0.1, 0, -0.1, …

13 -10, -7, -4, -1, 2, …

14 1.5, 0.9, 0.3, -0.3, -0.9, …

ISBN: 9780170354202

Finding *a* and *d* from an arithmetic sequence

In an arithmetic sequence, the first term is called *a* and the common difference is called *d*.

Example:

+4 +4 +4 +4

1, 5, 9, 13, 17, …

For this sequence:

$a = 1$ (the first term)

$d = 4$ (the common difference)

Find *a* and *d* for these sequences.

1 1, 6, 11, 16, 21, …

2 23, 18, 13, 8, …

3 3, 6, 9, 12, 15, …

4 7, 11, 15, 19, 23, …

5 120, 110, 100, 90, …

6 11, 4, -3, -10, …

7 0.5, 1.0, 1.5, 2.0, 2.5, …

8 18, 27, 36, 45, 54, …

9 5, 3, 1, -1, -3, …

10 ½, ¾, 1, 1¼, …

11 5, 5.5, 6, 6.5, 7, …

12 0.3, 0.2, 0.1, 0, -0.1, …

13 -10, -7, -4, -1, 2, …

14 1.5, 0.9, 0.3, -0.3, -0.9, …

ISBN: 9780170354202

Finding an arithmetic sequence using *a* and *d*

It is possible to find a sequence if the first term, a, and the common difference, d, is known.

Example: If $a = 2$ and $d = 3$, the sequence is:

+3 +3 +3 +3

2, 5, 8, 11, 14, …

Using the a and d given, list the first five terms of these sequences.

1 $a = 5, d = 2$

2 $a = -3, d = 2$

3 $a = 39, d = -9$

4 $a = 15, d = 3$

5 $a = 5, d = 10$

6 $a = -4, d = -5$

7 $a = 0, d = 12$

8 $a = 50, d = -5$

9 $a = 1, d = 0.6$

10 $a = 4, d = -3$

11 $a = 10, d = -\frac{1}{2}$

12 $a = 4.2, d = 0.05$

13 $a = 320, d = -80$

14 $a = -6.4, d = 1.2$

ISBN: 9780170354202

Finding any term in an arithmetic sequence

Any term in an arithmetic sequence can be found using this formula:

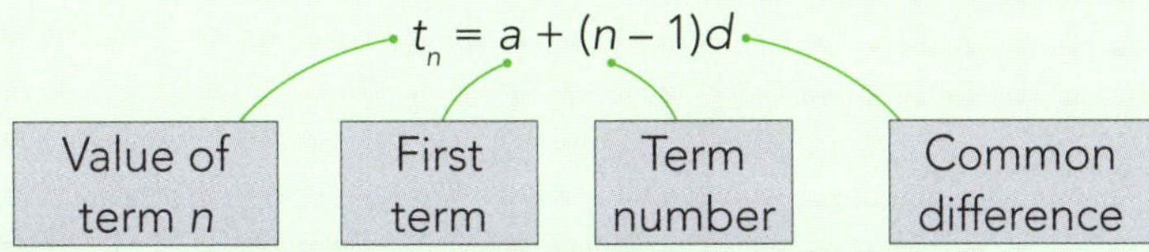

a stands for the first term, *d* is the common difference, and *n* is the term number you wish to find.

Example one: If $a = 5$ and $d = 2$, find the 100th term (t_{100}).
We could write them all out, but that would take a long time. Instead, we use the formula:

$$t_n = a + (n - 1) \times d$$
$$t_{100} = 5 + (100 - 1) \times 2$$
$$t_{100} = 203$$

So the 100th term in the sequence is 203.

Example two: If $a = 160$ and $d = -3$, find the 50th term (t_{50}).

$$t_n = a + (n - 1) \times d$$
$$t_{50} = 160 + (50 - 1) \times -3$$
$$t_{50} = 13$$

So the 50th term in the sequence is 13.

Find the required term for each sequence.

1 50th term of 1, 4, 7, 10, …

2 t_{11} for 10, 6, 2, -2, …

3 t_{20} for 3, 5, 7, 9, …

4 6th term of -6, 4, 14, 24, …

ISBN: 9780170354202

5 89th term of -2, 4, 10, 16, …

6 t_{19} for 1, 12, 23, 34, …

7 150th term of 3, 8, 13, 18, …

8 t_{11} for 100, 76, 52, …

9 t_{12} for 210, 195, 180, …

10 9th term of 1.5, 3, 4.5, 6, …

11 The 50th term of a sequence is 102 with a difference of 2. Find the first term.

12 A sequence has a first term of -5 and the 26th term is 70. What is the common difference?

13 Beka is a golfer who is starting a new training programme. She must hit 30 golf balls on her first day of training and each day hit a further 15 balls. How many balls will Beka hit on the 12th day of training?

14 Hemi's bank account balance is -$64. If he deposits $6.50 every week, after how many weeks will his account balance to be above $0?

ISBN: 9780170354202

Creating a general term from *a* and *d*

If a and d are known for a sequence, we can generate a general term (or formula). This will enable us to calculate other terms.

$$t_n = a + (n - 1)d$$

Example one: If $a = 4$ and $d = 5$, find the general term.

$$t_n = a + (n - 1) \times d$$
$$t_n = 4 + (n - 1) \times 5$$
$$t_n = 4 + 5n - 5$$
$$t_n = 5n - 1$$

We can now find any term that is required, for example:

$$t_{100} = 5 \times 100 - 1 = 499$$

Example two: If $a = 67$ and $d = -2$, find the general term.

$$t_n = a + (n - 1) \times d$$
$$t_n = 67 + (n - 1) \times -2$$
$$t_n = 67 - 2n + 2$$
$$t_n = -2n + 69$$

We can now find any term that is required, for example:

$$t_{20} = -2 \times 20 + 69 = 29$$

Find the general term for these sequences.

1 $a = 5$, $d = 4$

2 5, 12, 19, 26, …

3 $a = 31$, $d = -9$

4 1, 7, 13, 19, 25, …

ISBN: 9780170354202

5 $a = 7$, $d = 3$

6 18, 13, 8, 3, …

7 $a = 11$, $d = -7$

8 10, 20, 30, 40, …

9 $a = -2$, $d = 5$

10 -3, 9, 21, 33, 45, …

11 John's dad has offered him a new pocket money scheme. Each week John will get 50c more than the week before. John's first payment will be $1. Find a formula for John so he can calculate out how much he will receive on any given week. How much will he get one year later (in week 53)?

12 Alex is a farmer and she needs to adhere to new water restrictions. On the first of December she is allowed to use 10,000 litres of water. This quantity reduces by 150 litres a day. Find a formula for Alex so she can calculate how much water she can use on any given day. How much can she take on Christmas Day?

ISBN: 9780170354202

The sum of an arithmetic series

A **sequence** is a list of terms.
A **series** is the sum of the terms of a sequence.
The sum of an arithmetic sequence can be found using this formula:

$$S_n = \frac{n}{2}[2a + (n-1)d]$$

Example: Find the sum of the sequence 2, 5, 8, 11, 14, ... to 10 terms (that is, add the first 10 terms of this sequence).

$$a = 2,\ d = 3,\ n = 10$$

$$S_n = \frac{n}{2}[2 \times a + (n-1) \times d]$$

$$S_{10} = \frac{10}{2}[2 \times 2 + (10-1) \times 3]$$

$$S_{10} = 5[4 + 9 \times 3]$$

$$S_{10} = 155$$

Remember to use BEDMAS here

Find the sum of these sequences to the required terms.

1 1, 4, 7, 10, ... to 50 terms

2 6, 12, 18, 24, ... to 25 terms

3 9, 12, 15, 18, ... to 20 terms

4 3, 4, 5, 6, ... to 100 terms

ISBN: 9780170354202

5 -4, 5, 14, 23, … to 30 terms

6 2, 9, 16, 23, … to 15 terms

7 0.6, 1.6, 2.6, … to 10 terms

8 -45, -47, -49, … to 10 terms

9 -80, -67, -54, … to 50 terms

10 51, 48, 45, 42, … to 40 terms

11 Jemimah is training for a half marathon and needs to improve her fitness. On the first day she runs 3 km, on the second day she runs 5 km, and on the third day she runs 7 km. If Jemimah continues increasing her distance by the same amount every day, how far will she have run in total by the end of day 20?

 ISBN: 9780170354202

12 Dan is also training for the half marathon. On the first day he runs 0.15 km, on the second day he runs 2.9 km, and on the third day he runs 5.65 km.

a If Dan continues increasing his distance by the same amount every day, will he have run more than Jemimah by the end of day 20?

b On what day will Jemimah and Dan be running a similar distance?

13 Susie is training to be a netball goal shoot. She practises until she has put 10 balls through the hoop on the first day, 15 on the second day, 20 on the third, and so on. If this pattern continues, how many balls in total will she have put through the hoop by the end of two weeks (day 14)?

14 Hone is designing a large wall in a shopping mall, using black and white tiles. The bottom row has 152 black tiles and no white tiles. Each row after that has one fewer black tiles and one more white tile. If there are 47 rows of tiles, how many black tiles will he need?

Arithmetic sequence applications

Hints:

List the sequence before you start.

Beware questions that have a starting amount which is not part of the sequence.

Example:

Starting amount → 70 + (12 + 11 + 10 + 9 + 8 + ...) — sequence

Beware questions involving time.

Example:

t_1	t_2	t_3	t_4
2500,	2300,	2160,	1990

How much he had at the start (t_1)

How much *after* one week (t_2)

So 'after six weeks' means find t_7.

Complete these questions using an appropriate formula.

1 Janice works in a clothing store and her current pay rate is $13.50 per hour. For every month she works there, her rate increases by 25c per hour.

a What will her rate of pay be during her sixth month (t_7)?

b How many months will it take her to be on $20 an hour?

2 Arthur has 124 apple trees to prune. He prunes four trees per day starting on Monday and plans to prune every day of the week.

a How many will he have left to prune after Sunday (t_7)?

b On what day will he prune the last tree?

 ISBN: 9780170354202

3 A class of 28 students is saving up for a school trip. The teacher begins the saving with a $10 note. Each school day, every student contributes another 10c piece. There are 58 school days in the term. How much do they save during the term?

4 Aroha is creating a tukutuku pattern on a large panel with black crosses in rows. The first row has 8 crosses, the second 9, the third 10 and so on until the final row, which has 31.

a How many rows are there?

b How many crosses will she need to create in total?

5 A builder charges his clients a set rate of $80 for the first hour each day and $45 per hour after that.

a Write a formula for the amount he charges for *n* hours work.

b How much will he charge for a five-hour job?

c If he works seven hours a day for five days, how much will he charge in total?

6 Jules is building a brick fence. In the first hour she lays 22 bricks, in the second hour she lays 25 bricks, and in the third hour she lays 28 bricks.

a If this pattern is to continue, how many bricks will she lay in the fifth hour?

b How many bricks in total will Jules manage to lay in 10 hours?

7 Riley has a school essay to write. On the first day he writes 140 words. Every day after that he writes another 85 words.

a How many words in total will he have written by the end of the fifth day?

b What is the formula that relates the total number of words to the number of days?

8 Anna is making a patchwork quilt. She needs enough patches to cover a triangle. The longest row has 27 patches, the next has 25, then 23 and so on, and the final 'row' has one patch.

a How many rows will there be?

b How many patches will she need in total?

9 Find the sum of the odd numbers between 18 and 82.

ISBN: 9780170354202

Geometric sequences

A geometric sequence is one in which there is a common ratio, *r*, between consecutive terms. Each term is calculated by multiplying by this same number each time.

Example:

$$2 \xrightarrow{\times 4} 8 \xrightarrow{\times 4} 32 \xrightarrow{\times 4} 128, \ldots$$

The common ratio, ***r***, for this sequence is 4.
The next three terms in the sequence would be:

$$2, 8, 32, 128 \xrightarrow{\times 4} \mathbf{512} \xrightarrow{\times 4} \mathbf{2048} \xrightarrow{\times 4} \mathbf{8192}$$

An easy way to find the common ratio for a sequence is to take the second term and divide it by the first term. This is particularly useful if the ratio is hard to find (that is, it may be a decimal).

Find *r* and the next three terms in these sequences.

1 6, 12, 24, 48, …

____

2 27, 9, 3, 1, …

____

3 6, 30, 150, 750, …

____

4 5, 6, 7.2, 8.64, …

____

5 1, -3, 9, -27, …

____

6 -8, -16, -32, -64, …

____

7 4, 12, 36, 108, …..

____

8 0.5, 3, 18, 108, …..

____

9 64, 32, 16, 8, …

____

10 3, 15, 75, 375, …

____

ISBN: 9780170354202

11 The population of a meerkat family is doubling every year. The current population is 23. Estimate the population in five years' time.

12 A pendulum swings with an arc of 12 cm. The second time it swings, the arc is only 9.6 cm. If this follows a geometric sequence, how far would the next three swings be?

13 A tree grows 40 cm in its first year after being planted, and half of the previous year's growth in each year after that. How much does it grow in each of its first five years after planting?

14 Harry runs 2 km on his first day of training and each day he runs 1.1 times further than the last. How far does he run on each of his first five training days?

15 During a zombie apocalypse, two zombies invade a town of 100,000 people. If the zombie population triples each day:

a How many zombies will there be by the end of the ninth day?

b How many zombies will there be by the end of the eleventh day?

 ISBN: 9780170354202

Finding a geometric sequence using *a* and *r*

It is possible to find a sequence if the first term, *a*, and the common ratio, *r*, is known.

Example: If $a = 2$ and $r = 3$, the sequence is:

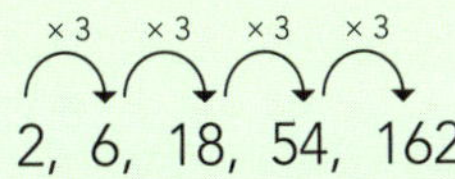

2, 6, 18, 54, 162

Using the *a* and *r* given, list the first four terms of these sequences.

1 $a = 5$, $r = 2$

____

2 $a = 18$, $r = -5$

____

3 $a = 3$, $r = -2$

____

4 $a = -6$, $r = 4$

____

5 $a = 150$, $r = 0.5$

____

6 $a = 15$, $r = 4$

____

7 $a = -4$, $r = 2$

____

8 $a = 5$, $r = 10$

____

9 $a = 1$, $r = 6$

____

10 $a = 8$, $r = 1$

____

11 $a = 1.2$, $r = 1\frac{1}{4}$

____

12 $a = 0.5$, $r = 0.25$

____

13 $50 increases by 10% per month ($r = 1.10$). List the first four terms of this sequence.

____

____

14 $50 decreases by 5% per month ($r = 0.95$). List the first four terms of this sequence.

____

____

ISBN: 9780170354202

Finding any term of a geometric sequence

Any term in a geometric sequence can be found using this formula:

$$t_n = a \times r^{n-1}$$

a stands for the first term, *r* is the common ratio, and *n* is the term number you wish to find.

Example one: If $a = 4$ and $r = 2$, find the 7th term (t_7).
We could write them all out, however that method would be long and time consuming. Instead we use the formula:

$$t_7 = 4 \times 2^{7-1}$$
$$t_7 = 4 \times 2^6$$
$$t_7 = 256$$

So the 7th term in the sequence is 256.

Example two: If $a = 128$ and $r = 0.5$, find the 10th term (t_{10}).

$$t_{10} = 128 \times 0.5^{10-1}$$
$$t_{10} = 0.25$$

So the 10th term in the sequence is 0.25.

Find the required term for each sequence.

1 10th term of 1, 4, 16, 64, …

2 5th term of 2, 5, 12.5, …

3 15th term of 2, 4, 8, 16 …

4 6th term of 14, 7, 3.5, …

5 8th term of 4, 12, 36, …

6 5th term of 5, 8, 12.8, 20.48, …

  ISBN: 9780170354202

7 10th term of 5, 15, 45, 135, …

8 7th term of 1, 5, 25, 125, …

9 13th term of 2, 8, 32, 128, …

10 12th term of 3, 6, 12, 24, …

11 10th term of 96, 48, 24, 12 …

12 16th term of 10, 12, 14.4, 17.28 …

13 12th term of 1000, 950, 902.5, 857.375 …

14 9th term of 8, 64, 512, 4096 …

15 A bacterial population starts at 100,000 and increases by 15% per day.

a What is the common ratio?

b How many bacteria will there be on day seven (t_7)?

16 The population of bees in a hive is 60,000. The hive is infected by a mite, which reduces the population by 20% per week.

a What is the common ratio?

b How many bees will be left by week five (t_5)?

ISBN: 9780170354202

Creating a general term from *a* and *r*

If *a* and *r* are known for a sequence, we can generate a general term (or formula). This will enable us to calculate other terms.

$$t_n = a \times r^{n-1}$$

Example: If $a = 4$ and $r = 5$, find the general term.

$$t_n = 4 \times 5^{n-1}$$

If *r* is negative, make sure you use brackets.

We can now find any term that is required.

Find the general term for these sequences.

1 $a = 5$, $r = 2$

2 $a = -4$, $r = 3$

3 $a = 3$, $r = -2$

4 $a = 1$, $r = 6$

5 $a = 150$, $r = 0.5$

6 $a = 15$, $r = \frac{1}{3}$

7 $a = 200$, increase by 7%

8 $a = 200$, decrease by 19%

9 Tiana's dad has offered her a new pocket money scheme. Each year, Tiana will get twice what she got the year before. Tiana's first payment will be $1. Create a general term for Tiana and then use it to calculate how much she will receive in the sixth year.

ISBN: 9780170354202

The sum of a geometric series

The sum of a geometric sequence can be found using this formula:

$$S_n = \frac{a(1 - r^n)}{1 - r}, \text{ where } r \neq 1$$

This means r cannot be 1.

Example: Find the sum of the sequence 25, 50, 100, 200, … to nine terms (add the first nine terms of this sequence).

$$a = 25, r = 2, n = 9$$

$$S_9 = \frac{25(1 - 2^9)}{1 - 2}$$

$$S_9 = \frac{25(1 - 512)}{-1}$$

$$S_9 = 12{,}775$$

Find the sum of these sequences to the required terms, rounding to 2 dp where appropriate.

1 5, 10, 20, 40, … to 5 terms

2 64, 16, 4, 1, … to 8 terms

3 1, 3, 9, 27, … to 10 terms

4 -3, -18, -108, … to 5 terms

5 4, 6, 9, 13.5, … to 12 terms

6 2, 10, 50, 250, … to 8 terms

7 3, 12, 48, 192, … to 9 terms

8 9, 18, 36, 72, … to 11 terms

9 5, -15, 45, -135, … to 7 terms

10 -1, 2, -4, 8, … to 9 terms

ISBN: 9780170354202

11 On the first day of his training, Gerard hits 104 hockey balls. On the second day he hits 156, on his third 234. How many balls will he have hit in total after his fourth training session?

12 Geoff starts his own business and earns \$2000 the first month, \$1200 the second and \$720 the third. What is the total amount that Geoff earns in the first 10 months?

13 A sequence is given by 34, 54.4, 87.04, 139.264, ... Calculate the sum of the first 10 terms.

14 The first term of a sequence is 125. If the sequence is increasing by 20% per term, calculate the sum of the first five terms.

15 The first term of a sequence is 125. If the sequence decreases at 5% per term, calculate the sum of the first five terms.

ISBN: 9780170354202

Geometric sequence applications

Ratios are commonly written as percentages.

Example one: Ngaire starts a new training regime. On the first day she runs 4 km. The distance she runs each day increases by 25% of the distance she ran the day before (that is, $r = 1.25$).
If Ngaire keeps to this programme, what is the distance she will run on the eighth day?

$$a = 4,\ r = 1.25,\ n = 8$$

$$t_n = a \times r^{n-1}$$
$$t_8 = 4 \times 1.25^{8-1}$$
$$t_8 = 19.07 \text{ km (2 dp)}$$

How far will Ngaire have run in total in two weeks (14 days)?

$$a = 4,\ r = 1.25,\ n = 14$$

$$S_n = \frac{a\,(1 - r^n)}{1 - r}$$
$$S_{14} = \frac{4\,(1 - 1.25^{14})}{1 - 1.25}$$
$$S_{14} = 347.80 \text{ km (2 dp)}$$

Example two: Sam is hammering a tomato stake into his vegetable garden. With his first strike with a hammer it goes 20 cm into the ground. Each strike after that makes the stake go a further 80% of the previous distance.
How far is the stake driven in the fifth strike?

$$a = 20,\ r = 0.8,\ n = 5$$

$$t_n = a \times r^{n-1}$$
$$t_5 = 20 \times 0.8^{5-1}$$
$$t_5 = 8.19 \text{ cm (2 dp)}$$

How far into the ground will the stake have been driven by the fifth strike?

$$a = 20,\ r = 0.8,\ n = 5$$

$$S_n = \frac{a\,(1 - r^n)}{1 - r}$$
$$S_5 = \frac{20\,(1 - 0.8^5)}{1 - 0.8}$$
$$S_5 = 67.23 \text{ cm (2 dp)}$$

Complete these questions using the appropriate formula.

1 Joseph is a keen runner. He wants to gradually increase the distances that he runs each day. If he runs 3 km on day 1 and he increases the distance covered each day by 5%, how far will he run on day 20?

2 Thomas earns his pocket money by doing chores at home. In Year 1 he spent 15 minutes per day doing these, and the time he spends increases by 10% each year. How much time will he spend on chores each day by the time he is in Year 13?

3 Caitlin bikes to school each morning. She sets herself the target of reducing the time she takes by 2% per day for two weeks. If it took her 48 minutes on the first Monday and 40 minutes on the final Friday, did she meet her target?

4 Chloe wants a curved flower bed. She plants rows of poppies with each row being 1.2 times the length of the previous one. The first row has five plants. She plants 10 rows. She rounds the number of poppies required for each row.

a How many plants are in row 10?

b How many plants will she need in total?

ISBN: 9780170354202

5 Hollie has started a new business selling ice creams. She notices that each hour she gets more customers. In the first hour she gets three customers, in the second hour, this doubles.

a If this pattern continues, how many customers will she have in the fifth hour?

b If Hollie closes after seven hours, how many customers will she have served?

6 Courtney is arranging squares to form a Fibonacci spiral pattern on her wall. The side of the first square is 2 cm long. Each square must have a side that is 1.618 times the length of the previous square.

a What is the side length of the eighth square?

b If she lined her squares up next to each other, how far would they stretch?

7 Jenny's rabbit has grown fat. It weighs 5.5 kg and she would like it to weigh 3 kg. She sets target weight losses of 0.2 kg for the first month, 0.18 kg for the second month, 0.162 kg for the third, and so on.

a How much weight should the rabbit lose during the sixth month?

b What should the rabbit weigh at the end of the sixth month?

c Will the rabbit ever reach the target weight? Explain your reasoning.

ISBN: 9780170354202

Dealing with time

When dealing with time, you need to be careful which *n* value you use.
Up until now, the problems have told you what happened in the first, second, third terms and so on, and asked you to find what happened in the *n*th term, that is, to find t_n.

Be careful of the following phrases:

after 8 years — this means find t_9
11 years later — this means find t_{12}
in 5 years' time — this means find t_6
at the end of 9 years — this means find t_{10}

They all involve finding a value after *n* years have elapsed since the first term (*a*).

Example: A population doubles every 10 years. If it starts at 20, how large will the population be after 50 years?

Time:	0	10	20	30	40	50
Population:	20	40	80	160	320	640
n:	1	2	3	4	5	6

Notice that what we want here is t_6, not t_5.

1 Gareth realised in Year 7 that he needs to spend one hour a night doing homework. Each year this increases by 15%. How much homework will he need to do a night in Year 13?

2 A youth group started with a membership of 35. Each year another 15 youths were added. How big will the youth group be at the end of the seventh year?

3 Nelson's new motorbike depreciates at a rate of 15% per year. If he bought it for $7000, how much is it worth in six years' time?

4 The height of a vine increases at 9% per year. Calculate the height of the vine at five years if it was 20 cm to begin with.

ISBN: 9780170354202

5a A grandmother put $3000 into a savings account for her grandson on his first birthday. It earns interest of 3% per year. How much will be in the account by the time he is 21?

b The grandfather also put some money aside at the same time in an account that had an interest rate of 2.5% per annum. If there is $5710.58 in the account when the grandson is 21, how much did the grandfather put in the account originally?

6 Rachel's new investment will gain 7.5% per annum. If 7 years later she has $8627.06, how much did she invest initally?

7 A farmer loses 2% of her crops a month to mildew and spoilage. If she originally has 65,000 tonnes, how much will she have in three months' time?

8 Walter's business makes 5% of its capital value in each of the first three years, then 12% for each of the two years following that. If his business is worth one million dollars initially, how much is it worth in five years' time?

9 Neil purchases a new car for $12,000. His car will depreciate at 18% per year. How much will Neil's car be worth in five years' time?

10 Trevor's student loan is incurring interest of 12% per annum. If his loan is currently $15,600 and he makes no repayments, how much will Trevor owe in three years?

11 Wendy left her dinghy on the beach and the tide has come in and swept it out to sea. When she first notices, it is 4 m from the beach. After two minutes, it is 1.5 times as far away. If this pattern continues, how far from the beach will the dinghy be in half an hour?

12 The volume of air in a giant ball reduces over time. It starts with 55 litres of air and reduces by 12% every half hour. How much air will be left in it after two hours?

ISBN: 9780170354202

Sum to infinity

It is possible to calculate the sum to infinity of a geometric sequence using the formula:

$$S_\infty = \frac{a}{1-r}$$

This can be calculated *only* for sequences where $-1 < r < 1$. This means the sequence is decreasing.

Example: Calculate the sum to infinity for this sequence:

24, 12, 6, 3, …

$a = 24$, $r = 0.5$

$$S_\infty = \frac{24}{1-0.5}$$

$$S_\infty = 48$$

Calculate the sum to infinity for these sequences.

1 48, 24, 12, 6, …

2 243, 81, 27, 9, …

3 96, 24, 6, …

4 6, 4.2, 2.94, 2.058, …

5 75, 30, 12, …

6 9, 6, 4, $\frac{8}{3}$, …

7 $a = 50$, $r = 0.75$

8 $a = 9600$, $r = 0.6$

9 $a = 1000$, decreases by 15% per term

10 $a = 4.8$, decreases by 70% per term

 ISBN: 9780170354202

Applications of sums to infinity

Complete these questions with the appropriate formula.

1 Donovan currently weighs 124 kg. His plan is to lose 6 kg in the first month, 4.5 kg in the next, and continue to decrease by the same ratio each month.

a How much will he lose during his sixth month?

____

____

b If Donovan continues to lose weight by the same ratio, how much will he weigh after a long period of time?

____

____

2 Mia plants a kowhai tree, which is 1.5 m tall. In the first year after planting it grows 0.5 m. Each year after that its height increases by 80% of the previous year's growth.

a How much does it grow after planting?

____

____

b How tall will it eventually be?

____

____

3 In a virtual safari park, a disease is spreading. In the first week, 500 animals die, in the second week, 400 die, and in the third week, 320 die. If this rate is to continue, how many animals would have died after an indefinite period of time?

____

____

____

4 Javier is learning to juggle. On the first day he drops the balls 156 times. On the second day he drops only 60% of the balls he dropped the day before. If this pattern continues, how many balls will he have dropped after a long period of time?

____

____

____

ISBN: 9780170354202

Arithmetic or geometric?

Identify whether these sequences are arithmetic or geometric by finding either the common difference (d) or the common ratio (r).

1 4, 16, 64, 256, …

2 5, -15, 45, -135, …

3 4, 8, 12, 16, …

4 4, 6, 9, 13.5, …

5 105, 10.5, 1.05, …

6 24, 40, 56, 72, …

7 44, 144, 244, 344, …

8 4, 7, 10, 13, …

9 6, 31, 56, 81, …

10 1, 12, 144, 1728, …

11 If $t_1 = 6$ and $t_5 = 66$:

a What kind of sequence could this be?

b Find the common difference and/or common ratio.

12 If $t_1 = 4$ and $t_3 = 13$:

a What kind of sequence could this be?

b Find the common difference and/or common ratio.

ISBN: 9780170354202

Mixing it up (applications)

Complete these questions with the appropriate formula.

1 A display of cans in a supermarket has a bottom row of 30 cans. The next row is made up of 28 cans, the third row has 26 cans.

a If there are 10 rows of cans in total, how many cans are in the top row?

b How many cans altogether make up the stack?

c How many rows could this pattern continue for?

2 Stacey buys a new car for $24,500. The car depreciates at a rate of 12% per annum.

a How much is Stacey's car worth after three years?

b In how many years is Stacey's car worth half the amount?

3 Mice have escaped their cages in a pet store and are reproducing rapidly. Initially there were 32 mice, and this is increasing on average at a rate of 10% per day.

a How many mice will there be at the end of six days?

b If this situation was left uncontained, how many mice would there be at the end of the month (30 days)?

ISBN: 9780170354202

4 A new theatre has 20 seats in the first row, 24 in the second row, 28 in the third row and so on.

a How many seats are there in the 18th row?

b If the theatre has 20 rows of seats, how many seats does the theatre have?

c The owners wish to increase the capacity to at least 1500, while maintaining 20 rows and 20 seats in the front row. Calculate a new value for d that would fulfil their requirements.

5 A seedling is planted when it is 1.2 m tall. At the end of the first year, it had grown 0.6 m. Each year after this the tree grew $\frac{5}{6}$ of the previous year's increase.

a How much did it grow in its fifth year?

b How much did the seedling grow in the first five years?

c How tall is the seedling after seven years?

d What is the maximum height that the tree will grow to?

ISBN: 9780170354202

6 Maggie is laying some irrigation pipes in her back yard. On the first day she lays 3 m of the pipes, but the job gets progressively harder each day and she only manages to lay ¾ of the length of the previous day.

a What length of pipes does she lay on the fifth day?

b What length of pipes will Maggie be able to lay over an indefinite period of time?

7 Pania and Wiremu are offered the choice of two pocket money schemes. They both start at $50 a month. The first increases by $2 each month. The second increases by 3.5% per month. Pania chooses the first and Wiremu chooses the second. Investigate both schemes and decide who is better off at the end of one year (12 months) and who is better off at the end of two years (24 months).

8 A swimming pool has a small leak and it loses 2% of its capacity an hour. If the pool originally had 31,000 litres of water in it, how much water would be in the pool after 24 hours?

ISBN: 9780170354202

9 A vineyard has 50 rows of vines. The first row has 12 vines, and each row has five more vines than the row before.

a How many vines are in each of the first five rows of the orchard?

b How many vines are there in row 30?

c If there are 30 rows altogether, how many vines are there in the entire vineyard?

10 When a pendulum is released, the distance it swings decreases with each swing. If the pendulum moves 60 cm on the first swing and each swing is 90% of the previous one:

a How far does it move during the eighth swing?

b How far does it swing in total by the end of the eighth swing?

c How far does it swing in total by the time it stops?

ISBN: 9780170354202

Investments

Investments may:
appreciate — become worth more over time
depreciate — become worth less over time.

Therefore $n = 11$

Example: Tama bought shares in a forestry block for $15,000. In 10 years' time, the trees will be harvested and it is estimated that the value will have increased by 8% per year. If the trees were harvested in 10 years' time, how much would they be worth?

$$a = 15{,}000,\ r = 1.08,\ n = 11$$

$$t_n = a \times r^{n-1}$$
$$t_{11} = 15{,}000 \times 1.08^{11-1}$$
$$t_{11} = \$32{,}383.87 \text{ (2 dp)}$$

At harvest time, some of the trees are found to be carrying a disease so Tama actually loses 5% a year. How much are his shares worth by harvest time?

$$a = 15{,}000,\ r = 0.95,\ n = 11$$

$$t_n = a \times r^{n-1}$$
$$t_{11} = 15{,}000 \times 0.95^{11-1}$$
$$t_{11} = \$8{,}981.05 \text{ (2 dp)}$$

Find the value of these investments.

1 Sandy invested in a house that cost $275,000. Each year the house is worth 4% more. How much is it worth in five years' time?

____

____

____

____

____

____

2 A failed investment of $50,000 depreciates at a rate of 5.6% per month. How much is it worth by the end of the year?

____

____

____

____

____

____

ISBN: 9780170354202

3 An initial sum of money is invested for 10 years at an interest rate of 12%. The investment is now worth $2,773.52. What was the value of the initial investment (to the nearest dollar)?

4 An investment of $3,500 is now worth $8,709.12. The interest rate was 20% per year. How long has the money been invested?

5 Angus has $10,000 to invest and he wants it to double in 10 years' time. Calculate the minimum rate of interest required for this to happen.

6 A new office block costing $10 million is about to be started, but earthquakes prevent it being built for another three years. If building costs increase by 8% per year, estimate the building's final cost.

7 Anna has $10,000 to invest for five years. She can choose between two schemes: scheme A pays 5% interest every year; scheme B pays 2.5% interest every six months. Evaluate both schemes and suggest which she should use and why.

8 Abigail's parents bought a house in 2000, which cost them $310,000. If they sold it in 2014 for $760,000, calculate the average rate of appreciation of the house.

  ISBN: 9780170354202

9 A partnership bought two new laptops at $1,300 each. The laptops depreciate at 30% per year. What will they each be worth in three years' time?

10 A car is on the company books at $13,800. Cars depreciate at 18% per year. If it was bought three years ago, what was its original price (to the nearest $1,000)?

11 An investment group buys a painting for $8,000 and five years later sells it for $7,050. At what annual rate has the painting depreciated?

12 Aunt Emily doesn't trust banks. Instead, she hides cash in a box under her bed. She put $1,500 in the box 10 years ago. If she had put it in the bank at an interest rate of 4%, instead of under the bed, how much more would it be worth now?

13 An investment of $10,000 depreciates at a rate of 2% per year for three years. It then appreciates at a rate of 4% per year for the following three years.

a What is the investment worth at the end of six years?

b Calculate the overall change in value over the six-year period.

ISBN: 9780170354202

Inexact sequences

It is unusual for sequences to have exact ratios.

Example: Kiri invested $10,000 in the share market. The value of her investment increased over the following three years:

Initial investment	First year	Second year	Third year
$10,000,	$10,793,	$11,830,	$12,772

$$a = 10{,}000 \quad r = \frac{1.0793 + 1.0961 + 1.0796}{3}$$

$$r = 1.085$$

That is, at 8.5% per year

If this rate continues, what is her investment likely to be worth after 10 years?

$$t_n = a \times r^{n-1}$$
$$t_{11} = 10{,}000 \times 1.085^{11-1}$$
$$t_{11} = \$22{,}609.83 \text{ (2 dp)}$$

1 A pregnant rat lands on a pest-free island and, as a result, the population of rats increases dramatically. The population is measured at two-month intervals:

1, 12, 114, 1049, 10595

a What type of sequence is this?

____

b Describe how the population increases.

____

c If this rate of increase continues, calculate the number of rats on the island after two years.

____

____

2 A car costs $15,000. Its value depreciates over the next few years:

$15,000, $12,900, $11,800, $10,200, $9,000

a What type of sequence is this?

____

b Describe how the value of the car is decreasing.

____

ISBN: 9780170354202

c What will it be worth after 10 years?

d After how many years will it be worth half the purchase price?

3 A fence is to be built beside a roughly sloping lawn, which is 50 m long. The top edge of the fence is to be horizontal. The posts are 2 m apart. The final (highest) post needs to be 2.5 m high. The heights (in metres) of the shortest five posts are:

0.5, 0.592, 0.674, 0.739, 0.824

The fencepost heights could be modelled by either an arithmetic or a geometric sequence.

a Describe how the fencepost height is increasing using each sequence.

b Use both models to calculate the height of the tallest post. Decide which is the better model and explain your reasoning.

c If each fencepost must have 0.6 m below the ground, use your preferred model to estimate the total number of linear metres of fencepost required by the builder.

4 Albert is saving for an overseas holiday. So far he has managed to save $850, $980, $1,119 and $1,310. Find the average ratio for Albert's savings.

ISBN: 9780170354202

5 A Thursday breakfast club is established at a school. Word spreads among the children and it becomes more popular. The following shows the number of pieces of toast eaten on each of the first six Thursdays:

18, 24, 32, 39, 45, 54

a There are 40 weeks in the school year. Use both arithmetic and geometric models to estimate the number of pieces of toast that will be eaten in week 40.

b There are 22 slices in a loaf, and each loaf costs the school $2.35 on average. Any bread left over from one breakfast is frozen until the following week. Estimate the total cost of bread for the first year.

6 These are the heights (in centimetres) of Ellie's cactus during the first four years:

5.06, 5.25, 5.5, 5.7

a Find the average ratio for the height of Ellie's cactus.

b Estimate its height in year 10.

  ISBN: 9780170354202

Practice tasks

Practice task one

Hamish has the option of either leasing or purchasing a car. To lease the the car would cost Hamish $800 for the first month, and this charge would reduce by $20 per month. To purchase the same car outright would cost $53,000, and the car would depreciate at a rate of 15% per year.

a Write a general term for the lease option.

b How much will Hamish have to pay in the 12th month?

c Calculate the total cost of the lease option after five years.

d How long will it take for the lease option to reduce to $500 a month?

e Write a general term for purchase option.

f If Hamish purchases the car, calculate its value after two years.

g Calculate the depreciated value of the car after five years.

h If Hamish had invested his $53,000 instead at an interest rate of 4%, how much money would he have at the end of five years?

ISBN: 9780170354202

Practice task two

Becca needs a new phone. She investigates several different ways of buying the model she wants, and she would like to know which method will be cheapest over the first two years.

Scheme A: She could pay $250 for the handset. In this case she would need to pay $49 for the first month, and $1 less for each of the following months.

- Calculate her monthly charge for the 24th month.
- Calculate the total amount she will have paid in monthly charges in the two-year period.
- How much will she have paid, including the cost of the handset, over the two years?

Scheme B: She could pay $350 for the handset. In this case she would need to pay $39 for the first month, and the monthly charge drops by 2% for each of the following months.

- Calculate her monthly charge for the 24th month.
- Calculate the total amount she will have paid in monthly charges in the two-year period.
- How much will she have paid, including the cost of the handset, over the two years?

- Which scheme would you recommend and why?
- Scheme A has a buy-out clause. At the end of the first year, you can pay a buy-out fee of $200 and switch to a $20 per month prepay scheme. Investigate whether this would be worthwhile.

  ISBN: 9780170354202

Practice task three

Basil and Blair have entered a hotdog-eating competition. The rules state that a hotdog is not counted as eaten until it is completely consumed.

Basil eats his first hotdog in 1.8 seconds, and after that each hotdog takes 0.3 seconds longer to eat than the previous one.

Blair also eats his first hotdog in 1.8 seconds, and after that each hotdog takes 1.08 times the previous one.

- How long does each of them take to eat the 10th hotdog?
- How long does it take each of them to eat their first 10 hotdogs?
- How many hotdogs will each have consumed in the first minute?
- The competition ends when one person has eaten 40 hotdogs. Who wins and how long does it take?
- How many hotdogs will it take before Basil's consumption rate exceeds Blair's?

ISBN: 9780170354202

Practice task four

Horace grows cabbages. He returns from a holiday to find that his cabbages are being eaten by caterpillars. He counts 12 caterpillars in one square metre of his crop. From experience, he knows that if he does nothing, the number of caterpillars will increase at a rate of 18% per day.

On the day of his return he harvests 200 cabbages for the market. However, because of the infestation, he knows that the number of marketable cabbages will reduce by 15 per day.

He orders a pesticide off the internet. However, this will not arrive for another 10 days. The company selling it claims that the pesticide will reduce the number of caterpillars by 39% per day.

- How many caterpillars are there per square metre by the time the pesticide arrives?
- How many cabbages will Horace be able to take to market on day 10?
- How many cabbages will Horace have sold in total by the end of day 10, assuming he sells all his cabbages?
- If the pesticide doesn't show up, how long will it be before Horace has no cabbages to take to the market?
- Immediately before applying the pesticide, he actually has 64 caterpillars per square metre. If the pesticide company's claims are correct, how long will it be before the number of caterpillars per square metre drops below three?
- In fact, it takes 15 days after the application of the pesticide before the number of caterpillars per square metre reduces below three. Calculate the actual rate of reduction of the caterpillars by the pesticide.

ISBN: 9780170354202

Practice task five

Introduction

A multimillionaire is looking at investing in two cruise liners. The number of decks and cabins to be built on each ship will vary. However, the multimillionaire wants to earn a similar amount of income from each ship. This assessment activity requires you to use sequences and series to describe the deck income and total ship income of each vessel, and to determine the number of decks on each ship so that they produce similar incomes.

Task

Working independently, use the ship descriptions below to make a recommendation to the multimillionaire. Include in your recommendation:

- the deck income for all the cabins on any deck in each of the two vessels
- the total income for each of the two vessels
- the number of decks that should be built for each vessel so that the difference in the total income for the vessels is no more than $5,000.

Catamarian

This is the plan for each deck of the *Catamarian*:

- There are 34 outside cabins on each deck.
- The outside cabins provide an income of $1,228 per cruise per cabin on the lowest deck.
- The income for each cabin on a higher floor is 6% more than the cabins on the floor below.
- The ship needs to be at least five decks high. However, it can't be more than nine decks high or it will be unstable.

Battalia

This is the plan for each deck of the *Battalia*:

- There are 36 outside cabins on each deck.
- The outside cabins provide an income of $1,055 per cruise on the lowest deck.
- The income for each outside cabin on a higher deck is $31 more than a cabin on the deck below.
- The ship needs to be at least five decks high. However, it can't be more than 11 decks high or it will be unstable.

ISBN: 9780170354202

Practice task six

Jack is planning to run a marathon. He will need to set in place a training programme in order to be able to successfully complete the course. Currently, he has a fairly low level of fitness, so he needs to ensure that his programme does not lead to any sporting injuries but will also enable him to build up to the fitness level required to complete 42 km.

Task

In this task you are investigating Jack's runs.

Programmes

One of Jack's friends suggests that he starts his training programme with a distance of 4 km, steadily increasing at a constant rate of 2 km per week. Another friend suggests he starts at 5 km and increases his runs by 16% each week.

Working independently, use the above information to answer the following questions.

- What distance will Jack be running for each training programme sometime after the fifth week (you select a week)?
- By the end of which week would the total distance he has run first exceed 100 km? (Compare both training programmes.)
- If Jack wants to be running 42 km as soon as possible, which training programme gets him there the fastest?
- Jack decides to undertake the first training programme and his friend Ryan does the second programme. By the 11th week Jack has run in total an impressive distance. How long does it take for Ryan to surpass him (within a kilometre)?

ISBN: 9780170354202

Answers

All differences and ratios are rounded to a maximum of 3 dp.
All other answers are rounded to a maximum of 2 dp.
Professional judgement should apply.

Arithmetic sequences (pp. 6–18)

(p. 6)

1 26, 31, 36
2 3, -2, -7
3 18, 21, 24
4 27, 31, 35
5 80, 70, 60
6 -17, -24, -31
7 3.0, 3.5, 4.0
8 63, 72, 81
9 -5, -7, -9
10 1½, 1¾, 2
11 7.5, 8, 8.5
12 -0.2, -0.3, -0.4
13 5, 8, 11
14 -1.5, -2.1, -2.7

Finding *a* and *d* from an arithmetic sequence (p. 7)

1 $a = 1$, $d = 5$
2 $a = 23$, $d = -5$
3 $a = 3$, $d = 3$
4 $a = 7$, $d = 4$
5 $a = 120$, $d = -10$
6 $a = 11$, $d = -7$
7 $a = 0.5$, $d = 0.5$
8 $a = 18$, $d = 9$
9 $a = 5$, $d = -2$
10 $a = ½$, $d = ¼$
11 $a = 5$, $d = 0.5$
12 $a = 0.3$, $d = -0.1$
13 a = -10, d = 3
14 a = 1.5, d = -0.6

Finding an arithmetic sequence using *a* and *d* (p. 8)

1 5, 7, 9, 11, 13
2 -3, -1, 1, 3, 5
3 39, 30, 21, 12, 3
4 15, 18, 21, 24, 27
5 5, 15, 25, 35, 45
6 -4, -9, -14, -19, -24
7 0, 12, 24, 36, 48
8 50, 45, 40, 35, 30
9 1, 1.6, 2.2, 2.8, 3.4
10 4, 1, -2, -5, -8
11 10, 9½, 9, 8½, 8
12 4.2, 4.25, 4.3, 4.35, 4.4
13 320, 240, 160, 80, 0
14 -6.4, -5.2, -4.0, -2.8, -1.6

Finding any term in an arithmetic sequence (pp. 9–10)

1 $t_{50} = 148$
2 $t_{11} = -30$
3 $t_{20} = 41$
4 $t_6 = 44$
5 $t_{89} = 526$
6 $t_{19} = 199$
7 $t_{150} = 748$
8 $t_{11} = -140$
9 $t_{12} = 45$
10 $t_9 = 13.5$
11 $a = 4$
12 $d = 3$
13 $t_{12} = 195$
14 After 10 weeks

Creating a general term from *a* and *d* (pp. 11–12)

1 $t_n = 4n + 1$
2 $t_n = 7n - 2$
3 $t_n = -9n + 40$
4 $t_n = 6n - 5$
5 $t_n = 3n + 4$
6 $t_n = 23 - 5n$
7 $t_n = 18 - 7n$
8 $t_n = 10n$
9 $t_n = 5n - 7$
10 $t_n = 12n - 15$
11 $t_n = 0.5n + 0.5$
$27.00
12 $t_n = 10{,}150 - 150n$
6400 litres

The sum of an arithmetic series (pp. 13–15)

1 $S_{50} = 3725$
2 $S_{25} = 1950$

ISBN: 9780170354202

3 $S_{20} = 750$
4 $S_{100} = 5250$
5 $S_{30} = 3795$
6 $S_{15} = 765$
7 $S_{10} = 51$
8 $S_{10} = -540$
9 $S_{50} = 11,925$
10 $S_{40} = -300$
11 $S_{20} = 440$ km
12 a Yes (525.5 km)
b Day 5 (11 km and 11.15 km)
13 $S_{14} = 595$
14 6063

Arithmetic sequence applications (pp. 16–18)

1 a $14.75
b 27 months
2 a 96
b Day 31
3 $172.40
4 a 24
b 468
5 a $t_n = 45n + 35$
b $260
c $1,750
6 a 34
b 355
7 a 1550
b $85n + 55$
8 a 14
b 196
9 1600

Geometric sequences (pp. 19–33)

(pp. 19–20)

1 $r = 2$; 96, 192, 384
2 $r = \frac{1}{3}$; $\frac{1}{3}$, $\frac{1}{9}$, $\frac{1}{27}$
3 $r = 5$; 3750, 18750, 93750
4 $r = 1.2$; 10.37, 12.44, 14.93
5 $r = -3$; 81, -243, 729
6 $r = 2$; -128, -256, -512
7 $r = 3$; 324, 972, 2916
8 $r = 6$; 648, 3888, 23328
9 $r = 0.5$; 4, 2, 1
10 $r = 5$; 1875, 9375, 46875
11 $r = 2$; 46, 92, 184, Estimate 736.
12 $r = 0.8$; 7.68, 6.14, 4.92
13 $r = 0.5$; 40 cm, 20 cm, 10 cm, 5 cm, 2.5 cm
14 $r = 1.1$; 2 km, 2.2 km, 2.42 km, 2.66 km, 2.93 km
15 a $r = 3$; 13,122
b 100,002

Finding a geometric sequence using *a* and *r* (p. 21)

1 5, 10, 20, 40
2 18, -90, 450, -2250
3 3, -6, 12, -24
4 -6, -24, -96, -384
5 150, 75, 37.5, 18.75
6 15, 60, 240, 960
7 -4, -8, -16, -32
8 5, 50, 500, 5000
9 1, 6, 36, 216
10 8, 8, 8, 8
11 1.2, 1.5, 1.875, 2.34
12 0.5, 0.125, 0.03125, 0.0078
13 $50, $55, $60.50, $66.55
14 $50, $47.50, $45.13, $42.87

Finding any term of a geometric sequence (pp. 22–23)

1 262,144
2 78.125
3 32,768
4 0.4375
5 8748
6 32.768
7 98,415
8 15,625
9 33,554,432
10 6144
11 0.1875
12 154.07
13 568.80
14 134,217,728
15 a 1.15
b 231,306
16 a $r = 0.8$
b 24,576

Creating a general term from *a* and *r* (p. 24)

1 $t_n = 5 \times 2^{n-1}$
2 $t_n = -4 \times 3^{n-1}$
3 $t_n = 3 \times (-2)^{n-1}$
4 $t_n = 1 \times 6^{n-1}$
5 $t_n = 150 \times 0.5^{n-1}$
6 $t_n = 15 \times \frac{1}{3}^{n-1}$
7 $200 \times 1.07^{n-1}$
8 $200 \times 0.81^{n-1}$
9 $32

The sum of a geometric series (pp. 25–26)

1 155
2 85.33
3 29,524
4 -4665

ISBN: 9780170354202

5 1029.97
6 195,312
7 262,143
8 18,423
9 2735
10 -171
11 845
12 $4,969.77
13 6173.90
14 930.2
15 565.55

Geometric sequence applications (pp. 27–29)

1 7.58 km
2 47 minutes
3 $R = 0.9799$, so she does meet her target of $r = 0.98$
4 a 26
b 129–130 plants
5 a 48
b 381
6 a 58.06 cm
b 148.77 cm
7 a $t_6 = 0.1181$ kg
b Weight = 4.5629 kg
c No, because $S_\infty = 2$ kg, so the rabbit can only reach 3.5 kg.

Dealing with time (pp. 30–31)

1 2.31 hours
2 140
3 $2,640.05
4 30.77 cm
5 a $5,418.33
b $3,485
6 $5,200
7 61,177.48 tonnes
8 $1,452,124.80
9 $4,448.88
10 $21,916.88
11 1751.6 m
12 32.98 litres

Sum to infinity (p. 32)

1 96
2 364.5
3 128
4 20
5 125
6 27
7 200
8 24,000
9 6,666.67
10 6.86

Applications of sums to infinity (p. 33)

1 a 1.424 kg
b 100 kg
2 a 2.5 m
b 4 m
3 2500
4 390

Arithmetic or geometric? (p. 34)

1 Geometric, $r = 4$
2 Geometric, $r = -3$
3 Arithmetic, $d = 4$
4 Geometric, $r = 1.5$
5 Geometric, $r = 0.1$
6 Arithmetic, $d = 16$
7 Arithmetic, $d = 100$
8 Arithmetic, $d = 3$
9 Arithmetic, $d = 25$
10 Geometric, $r = 12$
11 a Either arithmetic or geometric
b $d = 15$ or $r = 1.82$
12 a Either arithmetic or geometric
b $d = 4.5$ or $r = 1.802$

Mixing it up (applications) (pp. 35–38)

1 a 12
b 210
c 15
2 a $16,696
b 5.422 years (around 5.5 years)
3 a 56.69 mice (56 mice)
b 5263.8 mice (5263 mice)
4 a 88
b 1160
c $d = 5.789$, or at least 6 seats
5 a 0.2894 m
b 2.153 m
c 3.7953 m
d 4.8 m
6 a 0.9492 m
b 12 m
7 Pania: t_{12} = \$72, S_{12} = \$732
Wiremu: t_{12} = \$73, S_{12} = \$730.10
Not much difference at the end of one year.
Pania: t_{24} = \$96, S_{24} = \$1,752
Wiremu: t_{24} = \$110.31, S_{24} = \$1,833.33
At the end of two years, Wiremu is better off by about $80.
8 19,089.19 litres
9 a 12, 17, 22, 27, 32
b 157
c 2535

ISBN: 9780170354202

10 **a** 28.70 cm
b 341.72 cm
c 600 cm

Investments (pp. 39–41)

1. $334,579.55
2. $25,039.98
3. $893
4. Five years
5. 7.2%
6. $12.597 million
7. Scheme A: $12,762.82
   Scheme B: $12,800.85
   She should use scheme B because it earns about $38 more.
8. 6.6%
9. $445.90
10. $25,000
11. 2.5%
12. $720.37
13. **a** $10,587.13
    b 5.87%

Inexact sequences (pp. 42–44)

1 **a** Geometric
b $a = 1$, $r = 10.2$
c 1.268×10^{12}

2 **a** Geometric
b $r = 0.88$
c $4,177.51 ($4,200)
d 5.42 years (around 5.5 years)

3 **a** Arithmetic, $d = 0.081$
Geometric, $r = 1.133$
b 50 m of lawn will need 26 posts.
Arithmetic: 2.525 m
Geometric: 11.34 m
Arithmetic better with $a = 0.5$ and $d = 0.081$.
c 54.925 m (allow 60 m)

4 1.155

5 **a** Arithmetic, $d = 7.2$
Geometric, $r = 1.248$
Arithmetic, $t_{40} = 299$
Geometric, $t_{40} = 101,775$
Arithmetic more likely.
b $S_{40} = 6336$ slices, which is 288 loaves, $676.80 ($680)

6 **a** $r = 1.040$
b 7.20 cm

Practice tasks (pp. 45–53)

Practice task one (p. 45)

a $t_n = 820 - 20n$
b $t_{12} = \$580$
c $S_{60} = \$12,600$
d $n = 16$ months
e $t_n = 53,000 \times 0.85^{n-1}$
f $t_3 = \$38,292.50$
g $t_6 = \$23,516.38$
h $64,482.60

Practice task two (pp. 46–47)

Scheme A

- Monthly charge in 24th month = $26.
- Total monthly charges paid = $900.
- Over two years he will have paid $1,150.

Scheme B

- Monthly charge in 24th month = $24.51.
- Total monthly charges paid = $749.23.
- Over two years he will have paid $1,099.23.

Scheme B, because it is $50.77 cheaper overall.
The buy-out scheme is not worth it: $S_{12} = \$772$.
Adding the 12-monthly prepay cards gives $772 + 12 x $20 = $1,012.
Adding the buy-out fee of $200 gives $1,212, which is $62 more than the two-year total for Scheme A.

Practice task three (pp. 48–49)

- 4.50 seconds, 3.60 seconds
- 31.50 seconds, 26.08 seconds
- 15, 16
- Basil wins — he takes 306 seconds. Blair takes 466 seconds.
- 20 hotdogs

Practice task four (pp. 50–51)

- After 10 days there will be 53.23 caterpillars/m^2.
- Horace can take 65 cabbages to market on day 10.
- He will have sold 1325 cabbages by day 10.
- There will be no cabbages after 14.3 days.
- It will take
  $$\left[\log\left(\frac{2.999}{64}\right) \div \log 0.6\right] + 1 = 6.99 \text{ days.}$$
  So, effectively, seven days.
- Actual rate of reduction is
  $$\sqrt{\left(\frac{2.999}{64}\right)} = 0.8036\text{, so about 20\%.}$$

Practice task five (pp. 52–53)

Catamarian

$a = 41{,}752$ $r = 1.06$

t_5	\$52,710.94
t_6	\$55,873.59
t_7	\$59,226.01
t_8	\$62,779.57
t_9	\$66,546.34

S_5	\$235,359.91
S_6	\$291,233.50
S_7	\$350,459.51
S_8	\$413,239.08
S_9	\$479,785.42

Battalia

$a = 37{,}980$ $d = 1116$

t_5	\$42,444
t_6	\$43,560
t_7	\$44,676
t_8	\$45,792
t_9	\$46,908
t_{10}	\$48,024
t_{11}	\$49,140

S_5	\$201,060
S_6	\$244,620
S_7	\$289,296
S_8	\$335,088
S_9	\$381,996
S_{10}	\$430,020
S_{11}	\$479,160

When *Catamarian* has a height of six decks and the *Battalia* seven decks, there is a difference in income of \$1,937.50.

Practice task six (pp. 54–55)

First programme

$a = 4$ $d = 2$

t_5	12 km
t_6	14 km
t_7	16 km
t_8	18 km
t_9	20 km
t_{10}	22 km
t_{11}	24 km
t_{12}	26 km

S_5	40 km
S_6	54 km
S_7	70 km
S_8	88 km
S_9	108 km
S_{10}	130 km
S_{11}	154 km
S_{12}	180 km

Second programme

$a = 5$ $r = 1.16$

t_5	9.1 km
t_6	10.5 km
t_7	12.2 km
t_8	14.1 km
t_9	16.4 km
t_{10}	19.0 km
t_{11}	22.1 km
t_{12}	25.6 km

S_5	34.4 km
S_6	44.9 km
S_7	57.1 km
S_8	71.2 km
S_9	87.6 km
S_{10}	106.6 km
S_{11}	128.7 km
S_{12}	154.3 km

By the end of week 9 for the first programme and the end of week 10 for the second programme, Jack will have exceeded a total of 100 km.

The first programme gets him to 42 km by week 20.

The second programme gets him to 42 km by week 16.

By the 11th week, Jack has run 154 km (S_{11}); it takes Ryan 12 weeks to surpass him with 154.3 km (S_{12}).

 ISBN: 9780170354202